LIVE AT THE HOLLYWOOD BOWL

A RON HOWARD FILM
EIGHT DAYS A WEEK
THE TOURING YEARS

Cover image © Bob Bonis Archive

"Roll Over Beethoven" omitted due to licensing restrictions

ISBN 978-1-4950-8075-3

HAL•LEONARD®
7777 W. BLUEMOUND RD. P.O. BOX 13819 MILWAUKEE, WI 53213

Visit Hal Leonard Online at
www.halleonard.com

CONTENTS

TWIST AND SHOUT

Words and Music by BERT RUSSELL
and PHIL MEDLEY

Moderately, with a beat

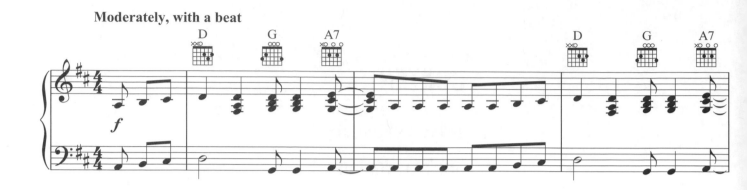

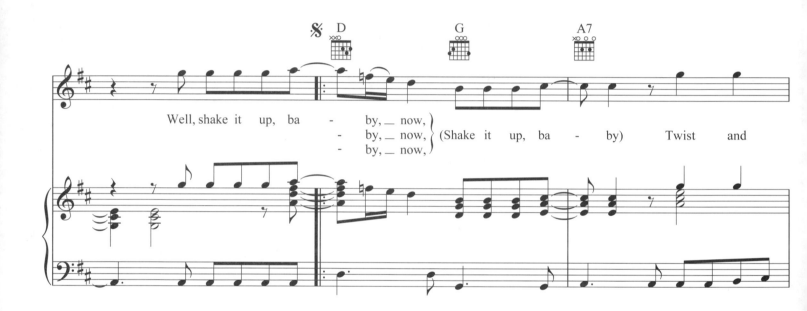

Well, shake it up, ba - by, __ now,
- by, __ now, (Shake it up, ba - by) Twist and
- by, __ now,

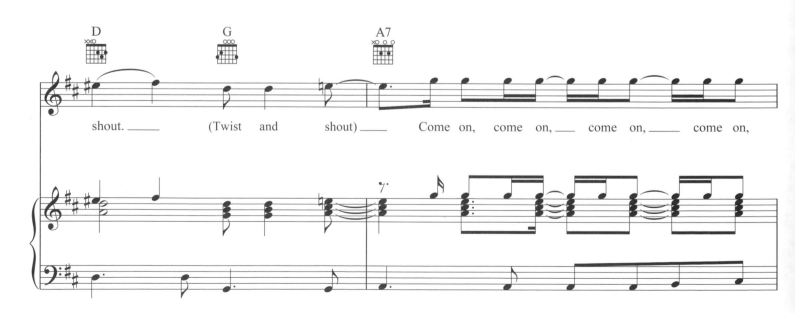

shout. ___ (Twist and shout) ___ Come on, come on, __ come on, __ come on,

SHE'S A WOMAN

Words and Music by JOHN LENNON
and PAUL McCARTNEY

Fairly bright, with a strong back beat

(1.,3.,D.S.) My love don't give me pres-ents,
(2.) She don't give boys the eye. ____

I know that she's no peas-ant.
She hates to see me cry. ____

DIZZY MISS LIZZIE

Words and Music by
LARRY WILLIAMS

Moderate Rock 'n' Roll

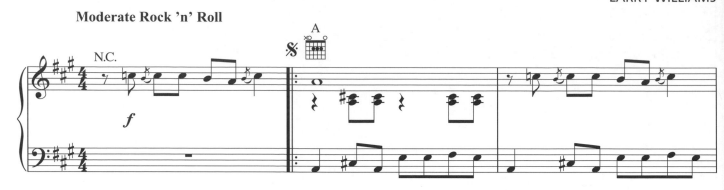

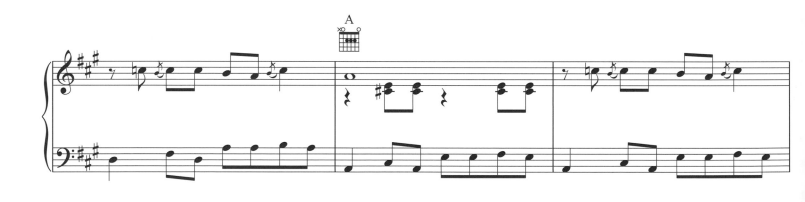

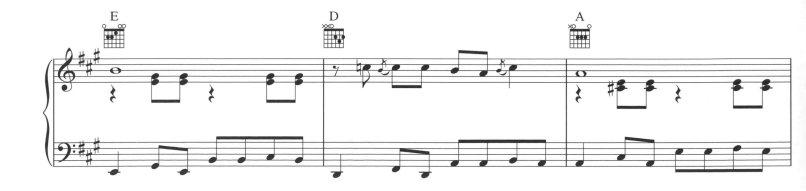

13

Come on, ___ Miss Liz - zie,
Come on ___ come on, come on, come on, ba - by, I
You make ___ me diz - zy, Miss Liz - zie, girl,

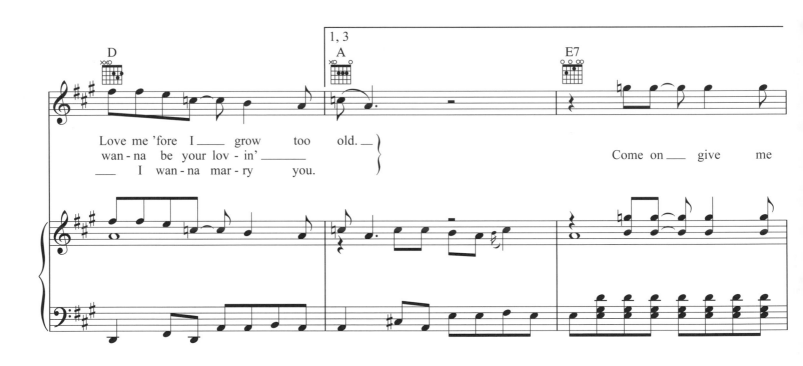

Love me 'fore I ___ grow too old. ___
wan - na be your lov - in' ___
___ I wan - na mar - ry you.
Come on ___ give me

fe - ver, ___ put your lit - tle hand ___ in mine. ___

TICKET TO RIDE

Words and Music by JOHN LENNON
and PAUL McCARTNEY

CAN'T BUY ME LOVE

Words and Music by JOHN LENNON
and PAUL McCARTNEY

D.S. al Coda
(take 2nd ending)

THINGS WE SAID TODAY

Words and Music by JOHN LENNON
and PAUL McCARTNEY

Moderately fast

BOYS

Words and Music by LUTHER DIXON
and WES FARRELL

Moderate Rock 'n' Roll

(1.) I been told when a boy kiss a girl _____
(2.,3.) My girl says when I _____ kiss her lips _____

take a trip a - round the world. _____
she gets a thrill through her fin - ger - tips. _____ Hey,

joy.   (Spoken:) All right, George.

D.S. and Fade on refrain
(take 2nd ending)

A HARD DAY'S NIGHT

Words and Music by JOHN LENNON
and PAUL McCARTNEY

Moderately, with a beat

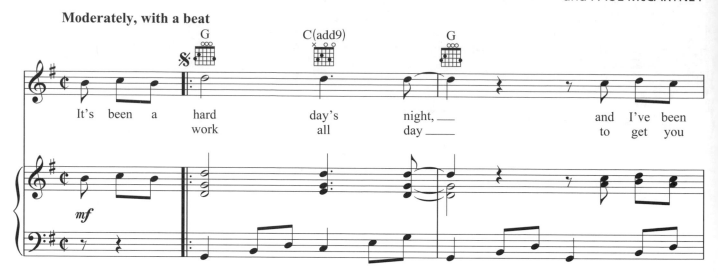

It's been a hard day's night, _____ and I've been
work all day _____ to get you

work-ing like a dog. _____ It's been a hard day's night, _____
mon-ey to buy your things. _____ And it's worth it just to hear you say _____

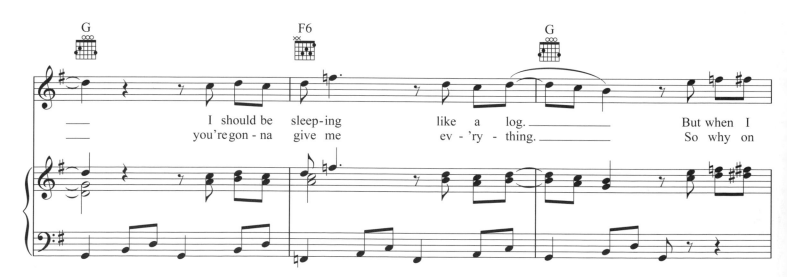

_____ I should be sleep-ing like a log. _____ But when I
_____ you're gon-na give me ev-'ry-thing. _____ So why on

ALL MY LOVING

Words and Music by JOHN LENNON
and PAUL McCARTNEY

HELP!

Words and Music by JOHN LENNON
and PAUL McCARTNEY

Moderately, with a driving beat

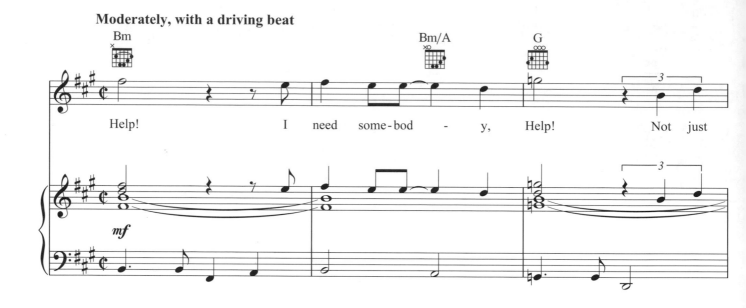

SHE LOVES YOU

Words and Music by JOHN LENNON
and PAUL McCARTNEY

Moderately

She loves you, yeah, yeah, yeah. _ She loves you, yeah,

yeah, yeah. _ She loves you, yeah, yeah, yeah, yeah. _____

You think you've lost your love? ___ Well, I

YOU CAN'T DO THAT

Words and Music by JOHN LENNON
and PAUL McCARTNEY

and leave you flat, _____

Be - cause I've told you be - fore: Oh, _____ you can't do

that. _____

LONG TALL SALLY

Words and Music by ENOTRIS JOHNSON,
RICHARD PENNIMAN and ROBERT BLACKWELL

I WANT TO HOLD YOUR HAND

Words and Music by JOHN LENNON
and PAUL McCARTNEY

BABY'S IN BLACK

Words and Music by JOHN LENNON
and PAUL McCARTNEY

EVERYBODY'S TRYING TO BE MY BABY

Words and Music by
CARL LEE PERKINS

Moderate Rock 'n' Roll

Well, they took some hon-ey from a tree dressed it up and they called it me. Ev-'ry-bod-y's tryin' to be my ba-by, Ev-'ry-bod-y's tryin' to be my ba-by, Ev-

(1., 2.) out last night, I did-n't stay late, 'fore I got home I had a
(D.S.) took some hon-ey from a tree, dressed it up and they called

nine-teen dates. it me. Ev-'ry-bod-y's tryin' to be my ba-by, Ev-

Went